LET'S TALK

Praying Your Way to a

Deeper Relationship with God

BILL CROWDER

Our Daily Bread
Publishing™

CONTENTS

Acknowledgments 7

Perspective 9

1. Dependence 13

2. Rest. 31

3. Acceptance. 49

4. Intercession. 67

5. Mystery 87

6. Confidence 101

Heart and Soul 121

ACKNOWLEDGMENTS

For me, few things offer a more staggering privilege and responsibility than being allowed to write. While my first love in ministry will always be the spoken word, putting words on a page has a sense of permanence that words floating through the air don't offer. Writing is both an exercise in thinking and a call to precision of communication—and that is the challenge. And when it comes to writing a book, more than one person and his thinking are required. It requires a team. A good one.

I'm grateful to be part of just such a team with the gang at Discovery House [now, Our Daily Bread Publishing]. Carol Holquist and Judy Markham have become dear friends and colleagues, as well as thinkers who demand my best. Miranda Gardner, as managing editor, pushes back in ways that make things better

7

than they would have ever been if left alone. The DH staff of David Frees, Dave Branon, Melissa Wade, and Ruth Watson support and encourage and remind me that I don't undertake this endeavor alone. I have company with me on the journey, and that is no small gift.

As grateful as I am for the team at DH, I am even more grateful for the team I have at home. Marlene, my bride now for more than thirty-five years, is the stable, consistent love of my life who knows when I am on track and when I am drifting—and knows how to call me back. I am also grateful for our kids and their spouses, Matt, Beth and Brian, Steve and Kimberly, Andy and Katie, and Mark and Kate—and for our wonderful grandchildren. For most of my years of following Christ, my family has often been at the core of my conversations with my Lord, and I have learned much about prayer as I have prayed for them and others God has brought my way. Those seasons of prayer have helped make this book a reality, and, for me, a necessity. Thank you all.

And to you, the reader, it is my deep desire that your own journey into relationship with Christ will be enriched as you think about your time with Him. Thanks for reading.

2014

PERSPECTIVE

In 1 Samuel 1, Hannah, a heartsick and broken woman, goes to "the house of the Lord" to plead her cause before the living God. As a woman of faith, she unloads all of her pent-up emotions, heartaches, and disappointments into a prayer that is so intense that a watching religious leader thinks she is drunk and accuses her of coming into the tabernacle of God in that state. But why, in her time of deep spiritual and emotional turmoil, does Hannah turn to God? Why does she pour out her soul in prayer to a God who must have seemed distant, silent, and unresponsive?

In Daniel 6, the prophet Daniel is under attack by his political enemies. Having thoroughly scrutinized his life, these adversaries have determined that the only way they can undermine Daniel's life is by attacking his devotion to his God. After manipulating the king into issuing a decree that outlaws prayer for a period of thirty days, these antagonists then simply bide their time, knowing that Daniel will not restrict his relationship with his God, regardless of the severity of the threatened consequences. So Daniel prays, fully aware of the price that will be exacted for his rebellion against the king's law. But why? What makes prayer so vital that he risks death rather than sacrifice his time of intimate fellowship with his God?

Throughout His life, as recorded in the Gospels, Christ repeatedly retreats to the invisible presence of the Father, bathing major turning points (for example, the selection of the Twelve) and major ministry moments (the raising of Lazarus from the dead) in prayer. But why? Jesus is God the Son. Why is prayer so necessary for the One who is equal to the Father in every way? Why is prayer so vital to Jesus?

If prayer is so important that it would overwhelm Hannah, cause Daniel to risk everything—including his life, and bring Jesus continually before the Father, why do we so often find it difficult? Why do we sometimes find it unsatisfying? Why do we struggle to experience the freshness and the wonder of our God when sincerely trying to enter His presence?

I suggest that many, though probably not all, of the answers to these questions can be found in one simple reality: perspective. Perspective enhances, transforms, and deepens our understanding so that even when our questions seem to lack substantial answers, we can still be drawn to God in meaningful relationship. It is my desire that the following chapters, which offer six of these perspectives about prayer, will illumine, challenge, comfort, and confront you with two overarching values: Who God is and why prayer matters.

This, however, is not intended to be a how-to book written by an expert on the subject. "Three easy steps to a meaningful prayer life" do not exist, and I join the journey with you as a fellow-struggler in need of wisdom and perspective. If prayer is as important as the Scriptures tell us, and as difficult as our experience seems to affirm, some fresh perspective may provide us with what "three easy steps" never could. It may provide us with a renewed desire to know and commune with "Our Father, who dwells in heaven."

Let's pursue this renewed desire together as we "talk about" these perspectives on prayer.

LET'S TALK ABOUT

DEPENDENCE

In August 2010, frightened wives and girlfriends, sons and daughters, mothers and fathers, supervisors and coworkers anxiously gathered above a copper-gold mine shaft near Copiapó, Chile, while, deep in the earth below them, thirty-three despairing miners huddled in the dark. Trapped 2,300 feet below in the mine shaft, they had no idea if or when help would arrive to rescue them from a slow and agonizing death. Then, on Day 17, they heard drilling overhead—drilling that continued until it produced a 6 ½" hole that must have seemed like a pinprick in the ceiling of the mine shaft. That pinprick, however, offered a speck of hope for those trapped miners.

This small, drilled hole was soon followed by three more drilling attempts, trying to find a delivery path for water, food, medicine, and rescue. These drilling operations were so vital that it is not overstating the case to say that those trapped miners were absolutely dependent upon those conduits to the surface, where rescuers had all the provisions that the trapped men needed for life.

Finally, on Day 69, the last of the thirty-three men were rescued—to the acclaim of the world and the joy of the Chilean people. Wives, families, parents, and friends celebrated the rescue while pundits and analysts lauded the indefatigability of the human spirit. But those men knew better. They knew how vulnerable and how desperate they had been. Without the determined intervention of committed workers on the surface, none of those miners would have survived, and they knew it.

This kind of story confronts us with the reality that we are extraordinarily frail. Human beings are "fearfully and wonderfully made," yet none of us can survive for very long in this world apart from provisions that are utterly outside ourselves. No matter how much it bothers us to admit it, the truth is that, like those Chilean miners, for all things in life we are eventually dependent.

The Reality of Dependence

It amazes me how quickly some animals can begin to function as self-sufficient creatures. When a colt is foaled, it almost immediately begins struggling to get onto its feet. Before long, that newborn colt is staggering to gain its balance, taking its first stumbling steps, and learning how to make its way in the world.

Compare this to human beings. We are the crown of creation—made in the image of the Creator, with souls and minds and hearts. Yet, at birth there is no creature more dependent than a human infant. It cannot fully and clearly communicate until it has been taught; it cannot eat without being fed; it cannot move from place to place but must be carried; it cannot defend itself but must be protected. In every area of life the human infant is completely at the mercy of its surroundings—unless there is a mother, father, or caregiver to protect it, feed it, carry it, teach it, and help it.

As a child grows and matures into a young man or young woman, however, he or she begins to feel the urge for independence. The desire to be free of parents, free of boundaries, and, ultimately, free of having to depend on anyone else for the needs of life is hardwired into our DNA. And this fierce desire for independence finds its roots in our ancient parents.

In the garden of Eden, Adam and Eve were
living in relationship with God, enjoying the
life He had given them and the provisions
He supplied for their well-being and survival.
Then came the sad, familiar story of their
disobedience and subsequent fall (Genesis 3).
Their fall, however, must be understood for what
it was: a human declaration of independence
from the Creator. It was a rejection of the simple
reality that as creatures we are terminally
inadequate, resulting in an actual dependency
upon our God and Maker. Thus, the heart of
humanity's rebellion was not merely a rebellion
against God's rule over us or God's rules for
us; it was mankind's rejection of the *need* for
God. It is the spirit expressed in William Ernest
Henley's poem ("Invictus," which declares:

> Out of the night that covers me,
> Black as the Pit from pole to pole,
> I thank whatever gods may be
> For my unconquerable soul.
> In the fell clutch of circumstance
> I have not winced nor cried aloud.
> Under the bludgeonings of chance
> My head is bloody, but unbowed.
> Beyond this place of wrath and tears

Looms but the Horror of the shade,
And yet the menace of the years
Finds, and shall find, me unafraid.
It matters not how strait the gate,
How charged with punishments the scroll,
I am the master of my fate:
I am the captain of my soul.

This poem is a prayer, but not a prayer to God—"I thank whatever gods may be." It is the poet's declaration that he does not need help from any god or any man. It is a celebration of the strength that he believes he already possesses: He is the unconquerable, independent individual. The author, William Ernest Henley, is described as an affirmed atheist, not surprising given the tone and spirit of this, his most famous work.

All of his bravado rings rather hollow, however. For like all of us, Henley would eventually grow weak and die. He was *not* the master of his fate, nor was he the captain of his soul. The inevitability of dependence that he had so eloquently sought to deny was, in fact, proven in the end.

This reality of dependence is, I think, at the very core of any discussion on prayer.

The Necessity of Dependence

Over the course of my years in pastoral ministry, it seems as if I have taught, heard, read, and discussed almost every imaginable aspect of the subject of prayer. Yet in all of our discussions and sermons and studies about prayer, what are we actually talking about? To that end, when engaged in conversation about prayer, I have often posed the question, "So, then, in your view, what is prayer?" The many responses I have received include:

"Prayer is interceding for others."

"Prayer is worship."

"Prayer is confessing to God when I have sinned."

"Prayer is making requests."

"Prayer is communion with God."

"Prayer is celebration."

"Prayer is giving thanks for God's provision and blessings."

"Prayer is asking and receiving."

"Prayer is . . ."

Dependence   19

And on and on and on come a variety of answers. But I would suggest that none of these descriptions really get to the heart of what prayer *is*. None of these answers is bad or wrong or unscriptural, but they fail to go deep enough. Why? Because while these are useful and accurate descriptions of how prayer *functions*, they do not really speak to what prayer *is*.

At times, prayer functions as an act of thanksgiving. Or, it functions as a season of worship, or of praise, or of confession. That is what prayer *does*, but it is not what prayer *is*.

It seems to me that, at its core, prayer is very simple. *Prayer is acknowledging our dependence upon God.* It is accepting in our own hearts and minds what God already knows—that *we need Him.*

This is pictured even in the physicality of prayer. When we pray, most often we bow our heads. We close our eyes. Sometimes we get down on our knees. We express physically what we must be ever mindful of in heart and mind: we are needy people who need God desperately. This is realized most completely in the act of prayer, because when we pray, we acknowledge something that is very difficult for people striving for self-sufficiency to admit. We are not big enough for life. With the very act of prayer we declare that we are inadequate, and that God alone is completely and eternally adequate.

And if life and experience are not sufficient to teach us our inadequacy, the Scriptures clearly underline this reality.

- Paul wrote, "Not that we are adequate in ourselves to consider anything as coming from ourselves, but our adequacy is from God" (2 Corinthians 3:5).
- Jesus declared, "Apart from Me you can do nothing" (John 15:5).

Now that gets my attention. We cannot honestly think that anything comes from ourselves, and without Jesus we can do nothing. Just as, in Christ's parable of the vine and the branches, the branches are totally dependent upon their connection to the vine for everything, so we are dependent upon God and His care and His supply. It is not our talent, our skill, our brilliance, our knowledge, our abilities or our personal charisma that get us through life. All those come from God, and every moment of our lives is in His hands. It is all Him—and that is a hard truth for our hearts to accept.

I am intrigued by both the name and the music of recording artist "Five For Fighting." The name seems to imply that this is a quintet (probably some mixture of singers, drums, keyboards, and guitars), but in fact it is one guy—John Ondrasik—backed by a revolving door of backup players. Actually the name "Five For Fighting" is a reference to a hockey penalty—five minutes in the penalty box for fighting.

Beyond that, however, is Ondrasik's music, which is thoughtful, contemplative, serious. This is especially true of Five For Fighting's most significant piece to date, "Superman (It's *(Song)* Not Easy)," which speaks of the frailty and weakness of even a superhero when facing the pressures of life in this complex modern world. The song was released in 2000, but it was after the September 11, 2001, attacks that the lament of the Superman captured the newfound sense of vulnerability felt by what had previously been seen as the indomitable Fortress America. In that season of questioning and grief, Ondrasik's woeful song was embraced as a cry of, among other things, the ultimate weakness and failure of human strength: "I'm only a man in a silly red sheet, and it's not easy to be me."

Like Five For Fighting's Superman, sooner or later we discover that life is too big for us. We are badly outmatched. We can never be strong enough. That kind of strength is not in us. It is in Him—and that is why we pray.

We are called to be people of prayer because we need Him desperately. And the sooner we embrace the fact that we are not Superman or Wonder Woman, the sooner we will begin to understand that this dependence is not a curse or a handicap; it is one of the greatest blessings we have been given.

The Blessing of Dependence

My friends Al and Sally are a bright, resourceful, educated couple who began attending our church at an age when they were beginning to anticipate their retirement years. Passionate for missions, they joined our short-term team that was going to Kiliya, Ukraine, to construct church buildings for new congregations of Ukrainian worshipers. Several days into the trip, however, Al suffered a massive stroke and had to be transported to a hospital in Vienna, Austria, for medical treatment.

What had, only days before, seemed like a "blue sky" future was suddenly turned inside out. Now, with Al's stroke, its effects, and the challenging prognosis, every day was going to be a struggle. Every day was going to be exhausting. Al had to learn how to do life differently, and Sal added full-time caregiver to her role as wife. It was a long, hard, and difficult path for both of them.

Yet today, fifteen years later, Al and Sally display a confidence in Christ and a deep sense of joy that is amazing. When the illusionary props of health and independence had been ripped away, they found that the God in whom they had put their trust was undeniably sufficient for everything they were facing or would ever face. A fresh resilience entered their hearts and their spiritual value system—a resilience rooted not in independence, but in dependence.

Dependence is often portrayed as something to be mourned, not celebrated. Yet it is through dependence upon God that we grow in understanding of our need for Him and the depths of His grace. Perhaps that is why the

Scriptures so often describe men and women being brought to the end of themselves—so that they might find all they need in Him.

Job lost everything.

Joseph was sold into slavery and unjustly imprisoned.

Hannah was tormented by her adversary.

David was pursued, first by his king, then by his son.

The widow of Zarephath endured famine.

Daniel was taken into captivity in Babylon.

Shadrach, Meshach, and Abednego were cast into a fiery furnace.

Mary Magdalene was possessed by demons.

An unnamed woman had an incurable disease.

Peter sank when trying to walk on water.

An unnamed man was born blind.

Paul lived with a thorn in the flesh.

In every case (and many more besides), these men and women cry to us from the pages

of the Scriptures that their seasons of struggle
ended up being cause for blessing. Why?
Because each of these individuals was driven
to the God of heaven who is sufficient. In fact,
as 2 Corinthians 12 recounts, when Paul prayed *Bible*
for relief from his thorn in the flesh, the loving,
merciful heavenly Father declined, saying:
"My grace is sufficient for you, for power is
perfected in weakness" (v. 9). *Bible*

Rather than lamenting God's refusal to
meet his need, Paul celebrated the sufficiency
of God's strength with these words: "Most
gladly, therefore, I will rather boast about my
weaknesses, so that the power of Christ may
dwell in me. Therefore I am well content with
weaknesses, with insults, with distresses,
with persecutions, with difficulties, for Christ's
sake; for when I am weak, then I am strong"
(vv. 9–10). Boasting and taking pleasure in *Bible*
weakness? It almost sounds unnatural, doesn't
it? Yet what a concept! Paul celebrates his
weakness because he now sees that it is where
God's strength can be displayed.

If we are to abandon ourselves to God's
strength, we must first be brought to the point
of recognizing our own weakness. Only then will
we acknowledge, live in, and grow to appreciate

the extraordinary blessing of being dependent upon God. It is the sound of drilling overhead that reminds us of how limited we are and how desperate we are. It is the compassion of God breaking through the stone ceiling of our self-will and independence to draw us to the true place of sufficiency found only in Him. It is the heartbeat of the prayers of the child of God.

A Song of Dependence

Five For Fighting's "Superman" acknowledged his weakness but had nowhere to turn for strength. How different the response of Annie Hawks, who turned the concept of dependence from a thing of lament to a song of worship.

> "One day as a young wife and mother of 37 years of age, I was busy with my regular household tasks. Suddenly, I became filled with the sense of nearness to the Master, and I began to wonder how anyone could ever live without Him, either in joy or pain. Then the words were ushered into my mind and these thoughts took full possession of me."

I need Thee every hour,
Most gracious Lord;
No tender voice like Thine
Can peace afford.

I need Thee every hour,
Stay Thou nearby;
Temptations lose their power
When Thou art nigh.

I need Thee every hour,
In joy or pain;
Come quickly and abide,
Or life is vain.

I need Thee, O I need Thee;
Every hour I need Thee!
O bless me now, my Savior,
I come to Thee.

—Annie S. Hawks, 1872

Years later she wrote, "I did not understand at first why this hymn had touched the great throbbing heart of humanity. It was not until long after, when the shadow fell over my way, the shadow of a great loss [the death of her husband], that I understood something of the comforting power in the words which I had been permitted to give out to others in my hour of sweet serenity and peace."[1]

"I need Thee every hour, most gracious Lord." Great words. True words. Honest words. Words of dependence. Words that form the song of our hearts as we cry out in prayer to the Father who loves us. Words that form more than a pinprick of a drill hole. Words that embrace the greatness of the God upon whom we so deeply depend—and the One to whom we pray.

Talking Together About Dependence

- Why do we often find it so difficult to acknowledge our dependence upon God?
- What elements of the human spirit contribute to such a strong desire to be self-sufficient?
- What experiences in life have been your "September 11" moments—moments that exposed your inadequacy and your need?
- Even the legendary Superman (cited in Five For Fighting's song) had to battle with kryptonite. What "kryptonites" do you face? How have you chosen to face them?

(Song)

---

1 K. W. Osbeck, *Amazing Grace: 366 Inspiring Hymn Stories for Daily Devotions* (Grand Rapids: Kregel Publications, 1990), 248.

- How did Al and Sally respond to instant weakness and dependency? What might your response be if you found yourself suddenly weak and needy?
- Why does God allow such experiences to invade our lives? What could He be seeking to accomplish through them? How might those things relate to the issue of dependence?

REST

As the TV commercial cameras pan into the kitchen of a middle-class home, they capture a familiar scene. Dirty dishes are stacked high in the sink. Laundry is barely organized in piles all over the floor. Several little ankle-biters are alternately eating their food, or throwing their food, or screaming about their food. The phone is ringing and the doorbell is chiming. The weary, exasperated, and fed-up mom lifts her hands to the sky and cries out, "Calgon, take me away!" Stressed and fatigued, she needs one thing above all else—rest. And the thought of a relaxing bubble bath seems the solution to her weariness.

King David might have sympathized with her desperate desire. He had been hounded by his son Absalom and hated by his former counselor Ahithophel. Having contrived a conspiracy to drive the shepherd-king from his throne, David's adversaries had marched into Jerusalem and established a new, albeit temporary, reign. For

David, there seemed to be nothing left but fear, despair, and a mad dash for his life. These are the circumstances that many Bible scholars believe set the stage for one of David's saddest psalms, in which he laments:

> My heart is in anguish within me,
> And the terrors of death have fallen upon me.
> Fear and trembling come upon me,
> And horror has overwhelmed me.
> I said, "Oh, that I had wings like a dove!
> I would fly away and be at rest" (Psalm
> 55:4–6).[B]

"I would fly away and be at rest." Not much has changed in the ensuing millennia. Exhaustion, burnout, mental fatigue, and a score of related symptoms seem to be increasingly "normal" in a world where we are pushed to our limits—and beyond. It seems that, along with our energy, our very life is being drained from us.

The debilitating nature of life in a broken world, however, does not go unnoticed by our Creator. When Jesus himself walked in the dirt of this world, He appealed to us:

> "Come to Me, all who are weary
> and heavy-laden, and I will give you
> rest. Take My yoke upon you and
> learn from Me, for I am gentle and
> humble in heart, and you will find rest
> for your souls. For My yoke is easy
> and My burden is light" (Matthew
> 11:28–30).

Bible
Bible

Notice that Jesus does not try to minimize the harshness of life. Instead, He candidly describes the challenges of life with two visceral, descriptive words: *labor* and *heavy-laden*.

These words speak specifically to just how difficult life is. It is hard, hard work, and in life we are often greatly burdened. That is why Jesus pleads with us to come to Him and to find in Him our source of rest. That, in part, is why we have been given the privilege of prayer. We saw in the last chapter that life is too big for us, and that, as a result, we are dependent upon God. But that dependence is only part of the equation.

Dependence takes care of the magnitude of the challenges we face. But if we are to recuperate from the effects of those supersized

challenges, we need rest. Jesus calls us to
himself and we respond in prayer—where we find
rest. In prayer, we not only engage with Christ
but with all three Persons of the Godhead who
work on our behalf to relieve us and help us in
our seasons of struggle and weariness.

This gets to the very heart of what makes
prayer such a gift. Often we talk about prayer
as the time when we "pray to God." While
this is not incorrect, it is incomplete. Prayer is
more than talking to God in a one-directional
monologue. Prayer is engaging with the three
Persons of the Godhead so completely that
prayer becomes more of a collaboration than
a soliloquy. Prayer is not something we say *to*
God; it is something we do together *with* our
God! This offers us three elements of rest,
residing in the three Persons of the Godhead.
The first of these three draws us directly to the
heart of the Father.

The Father's Compassion

She was an unwed, single mom with a young
son to care for. To make matters worse, she
had been abandoned by the father of her child,
left to fend for herself in a harsh and difficult
place where there were not a lot of options or

opportunities. Does that sound like something *(TV shows)* from an episode of *Judge Judy* or *The View*? Well, it isn't. It is the story of Hagar, the handmaiden of Abram's wife, Sarai.

Though Abram was called "the father of the faithful," he struggled (not altogether surprisingly) to believe that God would be faithful to His promise that, in his old age, Abram would have a son—the fulfillment of the Abrahamic covenant that he and God had entered into (see Genesis 12). *Bible* A primary part of that covenant was that through this son God would give Abram a lineage of descendants that would outnumber the stars in the sky (Genesis *Bible* 15:5). *Bible* But the years had passed and Sarai was aging. They were running out of time—at least on man's calendar.

So rather than trust God's promise, Sarai decided to use her maid Hagar as what we would call a "surrogate mother." She encouraged her husband to sleep with Hagar in the hope of producing a child through her servant (Genesis 16:1–4). *Bible* Unfortunately for Hagar, her resulting pregnancy brought about friction with Sarai, who began to treat her "harshly" (16:6). *Bible* This term describes what we would call emotional abuse; Sarai despised and browbeat Hagar. She treated Hagar so severely that she fled into the wilderness and sought refuge by a spring of water.

Consider Hagar at this moment. She was pregnant and alone in the wilderness, a cast-out servant with no means of support or survival. However, there, in her despair, she encountered the God of all compassion. The "angel of the Lord" came to her and commanded her to return to the tents of Abram and Sarai—but with a significant assurance. He promised her that not only would she survive, but her child would thrive and would, like Abram's promised child, produce an innumerable family of descendants (16:11–13). Then, the angel of the Lord instructed her to name her son Ishmael. (Ishmael means "God will hear," and this name provides us with the first of two powerful lessons about who God is and how He acts.

Hagar did not need to fear being abandoned or alone, neglected or forgotten, because the God of her promise is "the God who hears." Hagar then added to her understanding of God's concern for her by naming Him El Roi—"the God who sees." Nothing escapes His attention, for He is the God who sees and the God who hears. Hagar obediently returned to

Abram and Sarai and soon gave birth to her son Ishmael.

A number of years later God's promise to the aged couple, now renamed Abraham and Sarah, was realized and Sarah gave birth to Isaac—the child of the promise (Genesis 21). *Bible* This season of joy was marred, however, by Sarah's ongoing resentment of Hagar and Ishmael. The woman who had manipulated her husband into impregnating Hagar now demanded that he drive her away—and once again Hagar was in the wilderness.

This time Hagar despaired not only for herself but for her child. When her provisions were exhausted, she lay down to die with her boy, crying out to God, "Do not let me see the boy die" (21:15–16). It was a heartbreaking scene of *Bible* fear, pain, and unimaginable despair.

But, remember, the God she prayed to is the God who sees and the God who hears—and He responded to her heartache, provided for her need, and kept His promises. The angel of the Lord returned with words of comfort and challenge that called Hagar to put her trust in the God who had rescued her once and now would rescue her again. The God who hears responded to her cries, and the God who sees

opened her eyes to a previously unseen well
Bible (21:17–19).[B]

These evidences of compassion that pointed
Hagar's heart to the true and living God can
point us there as well. The compassion of the
Father for this woman and her child reminds
us that He is the God that David called to
"Vindicate the weak and fatherless" and "Do
Bible justice to the afflicted and destitute" (Psalm
Bible 82:3).[B] He is the God whose Son calls us to
trust, "for your heavenly Father knows that you
Bible need all these things" (Matthew 6:32).[B] How
does He know? Because He is the God who
sees and the God who hears. He is the God
whose compassion is as available to us today
in our wilderness seasons of life as He was
to Hagar in her fear and isolation. And that
understanding can give rest to your heart and
confidence to your prayers.

The Son's Intercession

When I joined the staff at Our Daily Bread
Ministries, I was given the opportunity to teach
the Scriptures in countries around the world,
and I embraced it with my whole heart. This
involved extensive travel, and the lion's share
of that travel was done alone. After several

years, however, this became more and more of a chore. Spending time alone in airports, airplanes, and hotels was compounded by seeing sights around the world that I would love to have shared with my wife, Marlene, but could only do so later, upon my return home, as I tried to explain what I had seen. At the risk of sounding like I'm whining, I grew tired of traveling and being alone.

Then, as our children moved into their adult years, Marlene was able to begin traveling with me. What a difference! Having her with me made an isolated experience a shared one, and seeing and doing things together dramatically increased the value of those experiences. Her presence made all the difference.

No one wants to go through life alone. John Donne rightly said, "No man is an island, entire of itself." Billy Joel, in his song "Piano Man," sees such aloneness from a darker perspective as patrons at a bar are "sharing a drink they call loneliness, but it's better than drinking alone." We were not made for solitude; we were made for relationship. We need each other, and intuitively we seek companionship in community. But this desire for community is not limited to human relationships. In fact,

it is fundamental to our relationship with the
Son of God. As we find rest and comfort in the
Father's compassion, so also we experience
rest through community with Christ—for two
significant reasons.

First, with Christ we know that, even in our
worst moments, we are not alone. In fact,
when we approach the Father to confess our
sins and failings, it is the Christ who comes to
our side. We do not face our wrongs and their
consequences alone, for Christ steps in as our
Bible great Defender. In 1 John 2:1 we read, "My
little children, I am writing these things to you
so that you may not sin. And if anyone sins, we
have an Advocate with the Father, Jesus Christ
the righteous." The word *advocate* is the key,
for it refers to what, in our day, would be called
a defense attorney. We can be at rest as we
confess our moments of failure because Christ
stands with us and for us.

Additionally, when we face the struggles,
needs, and burdens of life, we can know rest
in Christ because He engages with us in our
prayers. One of the great prayer-promises in
the Scriptures is based on Christ's intercession:
"He is able also to save forever those who draw
near to God through Him, since He always

lives to make intercession for them" (Hebrews *Bible*
7:25).[B] And the apostle Paul assures us that *Bible*
Christ is, at this moment, at the Father's right
hand, interceding for us (Romans 8:34).[B] When *Bible*
we come to the Father, we are not alone. The
Savior, who has promised His people that He
will be with us always, even to the end of the
age (Matthew 28:20),[B] joins us in those prayers. *Bible*

This excites me for a couple of reasons. First,
while we are called to intercede for one another
in prayer (1 Timothy 2:1)[B] and we know that this *Bible*
intercession is both a great responsibility and
a wonderful privilege, we do not engage in that
intercession alone. Christ himself is interceding
with and for His own. And second, we can be
at rest because in His perfect wisdom He will
always intercede with perfect knowledge and in
perfect relationship with the Father.

We don't need to labor or agonize over our
prayers. We don't have to be filled with fear or
anxiety in our prayers. We can be at rest when
we pray, for the Father sees and hears, and the
Son, who is with us always, perfectly intercedes
on our behalf.

The Spirit's Interpretation

As I mentioned, part of my responsibilities as a member of the teaching staff at Our Daily Bread Ministries is speaking and teaching at Bible conferences around the world, often in countries where English is not the language of the people. This means that over the years I have worked with many interpreters, and their skill has allowed me to teach in Russian, French, Malay, Bahasa Indonesian, Cantonese Chinese, Mandarin Chinese, Spanish, and Portuguese, even though I speak none of those languages.

In these teaching situations, my ability to communicate accurately and effectively is directly related to the skill of my interpreter. This includes skills in English, in the language of the country, and in the theological and biblical terminology that is a key ingredient in the teaching we try to deliver. This is certainly true of my Indonesian interpreter, Inawati Tedy. Ibu Ina, as she is known, speaks Bahasa fluently and has spent enough time in the States that she understands English, including American idioms. Beyond that, Ina is also a lecturer in a Jakarta seminary, which means that she also understands all the biblical vocabulary I need in both languages. When Ibu Ina is my interpreter, I can concentrate on my teaching, resting calmly in the confidence that I can trust her to translate the words of my mind and heart into the language of the listeners' minds and hearts.

That same calm and rest that comes from trusting the skill of an interpreter is part of the calm and rest we can know in prayer, for we also have an Interpreter we can trust. As Paul told the church at Rome:

> In the same way the Spirit also helps our weakness; for we do not know how to pray as we should, but the Spirit Himself intercedes for us with groanings too deep for words; and He who searches the hearts knows what the mind of the Spirit is, because He intercedes for the saints according to the will of God (Romans 8:26–27). *Bible*

Paul uses the word *intercedes* here, which is a form of the word translated "intercession" that we saw in Hebrews 7:25, but with a subtle *Bible* difference in meaning. While both the Son and the Holy Spirit intercede for us, here the Spirit's intercession carries with it the idea of interpretation.

   Notice that Paul says that the Spirit's
significant role in our prayer lives kicks in when
"we do not know how to pray as we should."
This addresses some of the questions that, as
a pastor and Bible teacher, I have often been
asked: "What if I pray for the wrong thing?" or
"What if I make a mistake?" or "Will the wrong
prayers be answered and my life be wrecked?"

   The truth is that God the Father knows
our hearts and He, as we saw with Hagar,
both sees and hears with perfect accuracy
and compassion. But the Holy Spirit helps
us in our prayers in a special way. Since
He perfectly knows the Father's will, He
intercedes for us by taking our prayers and
interpreting them to embrace the purposes of
the Father who loves us.

   Many times, through our experiences and
trials of life, we are filled with such anxiety that
we are driven to our knees in prayer. But our

prayer life does not need to be burdened with
such fears and concerns. In fact, we can know
a wonderful sense of peace and rest in our
hearts as we pray because the Spirit of God is
our interpreter—and He always gets it right.

A Resting Place

Just imagine this: the Creator of the universe responds to our prayers, and we find in Him, and Him alone, the rest we can find nowhere else. How?

- Because the Father, in compassion, sees and hears,
- Because the Son is constantly interceding for us at the Father's side, and,
- Because the Holy Spirit is interpreting our prayers in order to bring our hearts in line with God's good purposes for us.

The Godhead joins us in our prayers—what a resting place! And even though we still face times when prayer is agonizing and laborious, even in those times, ultimately, we rest in our prayers because we rest in Him. As the psalmist sang: "Be still, and know that I am God" (Psalm 46:10 NKJV).

Life is often filled with unexpected problems or crises. Unrest and despair can darken the way of even the strongest child of God. Yet because of the refuge we have in God, we can know stability in spite of stress and difficulties. As we are held securely "near to the heart of God," we find the rest, the comfort, the joy and

peace that only Jesus our Redeemer can give.
Because of this, we can live every day with an
inner calm and courage.

While pastoring a church in the midwestern
United States, Dr. Cleland McAfee was
stunned to hear the shocking news that
his two beloved nieces had just died from
diphtheria. Prayerfully, McAfee sought words
that would bring comfort to his grieving
brother and sister-in-law as well as to his own
grieving heart. From that came the words of
a hymn of consolation that have brought a
message of peace and rest to countless men
and women during the dark and overwhelming
seasons of life.

> There is a place of quiet rest,
> Near to the heart of God;
> A place where sin cannot molest,
> Near to the heart of God.
>
> There is a place of comfort sweet,
> Near to the heart of God;
> A place where we our Savior meet,
> Near to the heart of God.
>
> There is a place of full release,
> Near to the heart of God;

A place where all is joy and peace,
Near to the heart of God,

O Jesus, blest Redeemer,
Sent from the heart of God;
Hold us, who wait before Thee,
Near to the heart of God.

— Cleland B. McAfee

Hymn

As we abandon ourselves to our loving heavenly Father, aided by the intercession of the Son and the interpreting ministry of the Spirit, we can find, in prayer, a place of peace and rest—for, there, we find Him.

Talking Together About Rest

- When was the last time you wanted to run away from a painful or difficult situation? In retrospect, how did or how would running impact the situation? How did this affect your feelings and attitude?
- What are some of the things in life that make you feel weary? Which have you felt most personally? Most recently?
- In considering the "rest" we are to find in prayer, which action of the Godhead resonates most with you: the Father's

compassion, the Son's intercession, or the Spirit's interpretation of your prayers? Why?

- How can the Son's promise of His never-failing presence bring comfort in life's challenges? In your prayers?
- What do you think it means to abandon yourself to God? How might that help to produce spiritual rest?

LET'S TALK ABOUT

ACCEPTANCE

We all face watershed moments in our walk with Christ, and those moments usually, in one way or another, involve prayer. I faced one of those moments the night that our first son was born. My wife, Marlene, had been in labor for more than thirty hours when the doctor decided to do an emergency cesarean section because the baby was too big for her to deliver. As the doctor explained all of this to me, my first concern was for my wife—but I also feared for our child.

I was allowed just a brief moment to pray with Marlene before they took her into surgery, and then I returned to the purgatory of the waiting room where waiting was, literally, all that I could do. About an hour and a half later (around 10:00 at night), the doctor returned, and his facial expression was grim. I asked him about Marlene and he immediately assured me that she was fine—a bit groggy from being sedated, but fine. Then I asked about the baby.

"There's a problem," he said and began
to describe a condition that had developed
with the baby's lungs during the trauma of the
extended labor. He said that either the baby
would overcome it during the night and be fine,
or we would lose him—but there was nothing
humanly that could be done.

I was allowed a brief visit with a very groggy
Marlene in recovery and then was taken to
neonatal intensive care to see our child. I was
shocked to see our 9 lb. 8 oz. son in the midst
of all the tiny preemies—but they were all
equally struggling for life. After a few moments,
during which I was not even allowed to hold
him, I was given the direct-line phone number
for the unit and told to go home. I could call
in the morning and they would tell me what
transpired in the night, but, they assured me,
there was nothing to be done there. Home was
where I should be.

It was after midnight when I walked into our
little house, exhausted physically, mentally, and
emotionally. Alone in our home, I dropped to
my knees at our bedside and began to pray.
I prayed for our baby. I prayed for my wife. I
prayed for the ability to accept whatever the
outcome of this night would be.

At the time, I was a teacher at a Bible college. I knew theology. I could recite all the appropriate Bible verses. I understood the theoretical arguments regarding God's sovereign purposes and why it was only right to rest in them. But this was not theoretical. This was my son's life hanging in the balance. How would I respond if my prayers were not answered as I wanted?

At times like this—in harsh and unrelenting circumstances—there is no better example for us than our Lord Jesus in Gethsemane, where He modeled a key element of prayer—acceptance of the Father's purposes, no matter how testing or difficult those purposes may be. A careful consideration of our Lord's experience in the garden, where He wrestled with the cross itself, exposes some important principles for a meaningful pathway to acceptance in our own prayer life: honesty, determination, commitment, and resolve.

Honesty in Prayer

> Then Jesus came with them to a place called Gethsemane, and said to

Bible His disciples, "Sit here while I go over there and pray" (Matthew 26:36).

Let's face it. Most of us have been in one of those prayer meetings where someone hijacks the meeting. It is the phenomenon I have sometimes heard referred to as "stained-glass praying." The person begins to pray in theological language, perhaps interspersed with some Elizabethan *thees* and *thous*, and the longer the prayer goes on, the less authentic it feels.

Is God offended by theological terms? Is He irritated by *thees* and *thous*? Of course not. But the reality is that prayer is a conversation— and few if any of us would ever engage in conversation in that way. When speaking with those closest to us, we allow our hearts to be exposed and our lives to be vulnerable. And if that is how we converse with those who know us best, it certainly should characterize how we talk to the God whose care for us is immeasurable. Instead of flowery oratory, our conversations with God should be marked by the genuineness of honesty and transparency. Why do honesty and transparency matter in prayer? The simplest answer is that God

already knows the true condition of our hearts;
He is not deceived or impressed by spiritual
language or churchy jargon.

The prayers of King David were marked by
just such honesty. When he was pursued by
Saul and later by Absalom, David's prayers were
deeply emotional—filled with disappointment,
fear, and doubt. He did not fear baring his soul
to his God, and frequently prayed in ways that
displayed a depth of transparency with God that
we can actually find unsettling. For example, the
level of candor David expressed in Psalm 142 *Bible*
feels very different from the religious political
correctness that tries to frame prayers into neat,
easy packages. He declared:

> I cry aloud with my voice to the LORD;
> I make supplication with my voice
>   to the LORD.
> I pour out my complaint before Him;
> I declare my trouble before Him.
> When my spirit was overwhelmed within me,
> You knew my path.
> In the way where I walk
> They have hidden a trap for me.
> Look to the right and see;
> For there is no one who regards me;

Bible
> There is no escape for me;
> No one cares for my soul (Psalm 142:1–4).[B]

This transparency of heart is not limited to David's prayers. Christ himself modeled that in the garden of Gethsemane. As He anticipated the anguish of the cross, He said to His disciples, "My soul is deeply grieved, to the *Bible* point of death" (Matthew 26:38).[B]

Bible "And He went a little beyond them, and fell on His face and prayed, saying, 'My Father, if it is possible, let this cup pass from Me; yet not *Bible* as I will, but as You will'" (Matthew 26:39).[B]

No lofty words of piety here. No bravado to impress any who might have overheard Him. With brutal honesty Christ bared His soul to His Father.

Determination in Prayer

Bible
> He went a little beyond them, and fell on His face and prayed, saying, "My Father, if it is possible, let this cup pass from Me; yet not as I will, but as You will" (Matthew 26:39).[B]

movie One of my favorite scenes in the film *Chariots of Fire* has soon-to-be Olympic sprinter and missionary to China Eric Liddell running in a race. When one of his competitors knocks him off balance and off the track, the pack runs away from him, seemingly ending his chances of winning the race. Then, Liddell pulls himself to his feet and begins to run. The look of sheer determination on his face never wanes, and eventually he catches the pack of runners ahead of him. Refusing to give up, Liddell sees his persistence pay off as he wins the race—a race he could have easily quit.

Determination and persistence are also important elements in prayer. Jesus told important stories about individuals who evidence this vital characteristic, portraying them as people who don't lose heart. Luke's gospel opens one such story this way: "Now He was telling them a parable to show that at all times they ought to pray and not to lose heart" (Luke 18:1). Pray at all times . . . don't lose heart. That is a formula for persistence. And the widow in the parable that follows (vv. 2–8), who refuses to give up, becomes Jesus's call to us to not be afraid to approach our God with a high level of determination as we pray.

On this subject, however, one reminder is important. We may engage God in prayer that

Bible

is marked by *persistence* (as Jesus called it in Luke 11:8), but that determination must always be tempered by resolute trust in God's gracious purposes.

In the garden, Jesus balanced these perfectly when He prayed both determinedly and persistently (three times) that the cup of sin and judgment that awaited Him on the cross would pass from Him. Nevertheless, each of those three prayers was tempered by phrases like *"If it is possible"* and *"Not as I will, but as You will."*

As we will see in a later chapter, prayer is not a subordinate going defiantly to his or her commanding officer for marching orders, come what may. We go to the Father who loves us more than anyone loves us. This relationship must be at the core of how we pray, for it is in prayer that we see Him as the God who allows us to express our whole heart, soul, and mind to Him, as well as the Father we can trust to have our best interest in His purposes—even when our prayers are not answered as we wish.

Commitment in Prayer

Now an angel from heaven appeared to Him, strengthening Him. And being

in agony He was praying very fer-
vently; and His sweat became like
drops of blood, falling down upon the
ground (Luke 22:43–44).[B]   *Bible*

During a teaching trip I led to the land of
Israel, we visited all the usual sites (Mount
Carmel, Bethlehem, Nazareth, and more), but
one of the more instructive stops we made
was at the Galilean village of Tabgha. What I
found so helpful when we visited there was
the ancient olive press made from the volcanic
basalt rock of that region. The press consists
of a tray cut into the stone with drains that flow
from a basin into which the olives were placed.
Then, a large stone, shaped into the form of a
wheel, would be rolled around that basin until all
of the olives had been crushed under its weight,
releasing the precious oil that was so vital to
ancient Israel's life and culture.

This lesson on olive presses became
extremely important for our group a few days
later when we began to trace the steps of Christ
in His passion—and we began at the garden of
Gethsemane. When Christ entered the garden
of Gethsemane to pray, He was not entering the
type of garden we think of when we hear the

word. It was actually an orchard—an orchard of olive trees that still stands today, although today's trees appear to have grown from the ancient roots of the trees Jesus would have moved among that night. Furthermore, the name *Gethsemane* means "olive press." Thus, the very name of the place where Christ prayed is descriptive of what He endured there as He was crushed under the weight of the sins of the world.

Luke, the physician and writer of the gospel of Luke, goes to great lengths to describe the agony the Savior endured during His time of prayer in that garden. His anguish was so intense that an angel was dispatched to strengthen Him for the task that was to come. No one understood the Father's purposes better than the Son, yet He still prayed for the possibility of release. He knew that the redemption of a broken world was hanging in the balance, but He also fully understood and felt the horror of what that redemption would cost—physically, emotionally, and spiritually.

This powerful modeling of prayer reminds us that communion with the God of the universe is not something to be taken lightly. In the place of the olive press, only total commitment will do—for that is what is required if we are to genuinely wrestle with the divine purposes that we question and the life experiences that cause us to shudder in apprehensive fear.

Not once, not twice, but three times Jesus poured out His anguish and heartache to the Father. Three times He prayed that He might not have to walk this path. Three times He yielded His heart and spirit to the Father's will.

> And He came to the disciples and found them sleeping, and said to Peter, "So, you men could not keep watch with Me for one hour? Keep watching and praying that you may not enter into temptation; the spirit is willing, but the flesh is weak."
>
> He went away again a second time and prayed, saying, "My Father, if this cannot pass away unless I drink it, Your will be done." Again He came and found them sleeping, for their eyes were heavy. And He left them again, and went away and prayed a third time, saying the same thing once more (Matthew 26:40–44).[B]   *Bible*

Three times. Perhaps that was the example Paul was following when he wrestled with God in prayer over his "thorn in the flesh." This undefined source of struggle was not something that could be settled by having a brief chat with the Savior. It could only be dealt with as Paul fully engaged with the God of his heart, committed to whatever His purposes might be.

It is the honest expressions of our heart and a resolve to accept the good purposes of our good God that see us through life's darkest moments.

Resolve in Prayer

> Then He came to the disciples and said to them, "Are you still sleeping and resting? Behold, the hour is at hand and the Son of Man is being betrayed into the hands of sinners. Get up, let us be going; behold, the one who betrays Me is at hand!" (Matthew 26:45–46).

When Judas entered the garden with an army, apparently numbering in the hundreds, Jesus had completed His most critical time of prayer. Not surprisingly, He did not cower in a dark corner of the garden. He did not conceal himself behind the olive press or look for an escape through a back gate. Resolved—not resigned—Jesus went to meet His betrayer and all that awaited Him.

What we see here is not passive resignation—"whatever will be will be"—born out of a sense of helplessness and hopelessness. This is resolve, which comes from an encounter with the Father who strengthens us for whatever we must face—with confident assurance that His will and His ways really are best. Even when we don't understand them.

The cup was not taken from Christ, but He entrusted himself to the Father. Paul's thorn in the flesh was not removed, but through it he learned the power of a grace-filled life.

It is this resolve that can carry us in the times when life is hard, when circumstances are painful, and when our questions seem to go unanswered. The resolve to trust is a supernatural supply when faith seems to make little or no sense.

Acceptance and Peace

I am fully aware that any experience, challenge, or heartache that I have suffered or may yet endure does not begin to approach what Christ endured for us in Gethsemane.

and on the cross. But my moments of fear and
struggle do not need to approach His sufferings
in order for them to be more than enough to
test my heart, my faith, and my willingness
to trust in and accept the purposes of God—
whether I understand them or not. Peace does
not come from getting our way but by resting
in His purposes. And, without question, prayers
rooted in the example of Christ and His honesty,
determination, commitment, and resolve put us
in a position to accept God's purposes. He has
welcomed us into His presence. He has heard
our hearts. He responds with what He knows
is best, and we can trust Him. Even when we
suffer and we don't understand why.

That night more than thirty years ago, as our
baby fought for his life in the neonatal intensive
care unit and I prayed by our bedside, I came
to understand two things that I might never
have grasped any other way. First, I discovered
the amazing transaction that takes place when
you see your child for the first time. At that
moment an extraordinary bond of love swells
in your heart for this tiny person you have
never seen before and with whom you cannot
communicate. And at that moment you realize
you would give everything for your child. You

would gladly take his place and shoulder any yet-to-be-determined outcome of the suffering he is enduring.

The other thing I learned was how desperately you cling to God when life is spinning out of control. When that happens, you either trust God or you don't—and that is what makes those experiences such defining moments. All the stuff that I waxed eloquent about in my Bible college classes was being tested in the furnace of fear and despair.

So I prayed. In fact, I prayed until about 3:00 in the morning, when I had a deep sense of peace that all would be well. I did not know whether my desire would be fulfilled—that our child would live—but I did sense that, whatever happened, all would be well. Still fully clothed, I crawled into bed and feel asleep from exhaustion.

When I awoke about 6:30 that morning, I immediately called the neonatal unit to find out what had happened during the night. The medical person who answered the phone said, "It was the strangest thing. About 3:00 he made a turn for the better and all is well. Your son is going to be fine."

I would like to tell you that I would have responded with wisdom, grace, and trust had our son not recovered. I would like to but I can't. I simply don't know what I would have done. What I do know is that, more than thirty years later, we are still praying for him. His name is Matt and he serves in the US Army, which is more than enough to keep us praying.

That is my story of acceptance. It is imperfect and flawed, just as I am. But it is my story. And through it I discovered why the words to the classic hymn "Great Is Thy Faithfulness" grip my heart so deeply anytime I find myself singing it in a worship service:

> Pardon for sin and a peace that endureth,
> Thy own dear presence to cheer and to
>   guide;
> Strength for today and bright hope for
>   tomorrow,
> Blessings all mine, with ten thousand
>   beside.
>
> —Thomas O. Chisholm

Acceptance is much more about "strength for today and bright hope for tomorrow" than it is about "blessings all mine." But that's okay. In fact, that peace is the very fruit of accepting the good purposes of <u>God</u> in the season of testing—as our <u>Lord</u> did. As <u>Paul</u> did. As we can.

Talking Together About Acceptance

- Few biblical events are more filled with anguish than <u>Christ</u>'s experience in the garden of <u>Gethsemane</u>. As you consider what <u>He</u> endured there, how do you think <u>His</u> pattern of prayer offers guidance for our prayers during the worst times of life?
- Think about the contrasting elements of <u>Christ</u>'s prayer: A deep desire for the cup of suffering to pass contrasted with <u>His</u> willing submission to accept that cup. Why do we often find it hard to strike a balance between those opposites—our desires versus <u>God</u>'s purposes? What might be an example from your own experience?
- What parallels do you see between <u>Jesus</u>'s prayers in <u>Gethsemane</u> and <u>Paul</u>'s "thorn in the flesh" prayers in <u>2 Corinthians 12? How Bible do those parallels help us in our own times of thorny difficulty?
- How does resolve differ from resignation? Which do you tend to gravitate to? Why?

LET'S TALK ABOUT

INTERCESSION

Marlene and I have five children, four sons and one daughter, who are now adults. When our kids were younger, however, Marlene was determined that each of them was going to be taught how to find their way around a kitchen. She taught them how to cook basic meals (and some not-so-basic meals) as well as the fundamentals of baking. In doing this, she did not sit them down to watch the Food Network or simply hand them a recipe book and tell them to figure it out on their own. No, she taught them by showing them how to prepare many types of dishes. They needed to learn about the various ingredients a recipe called for, what spices or seasonings were to be used and why, how to make sense of the measurements required, and the difference between stirring in ingredients and folding in ingredients. It was a lengthy process, and she made it fun, with the wonderful reward of something special for everyone to enjoy—fresh from the stove or the oven. To this day, all five of our kids can hold

their own (or better) in the kitchen because
Marlene invested the time necessary to teach
them how. And she did not teach by words
alone; she taught by example.

This need for a proper example applies
to prayer as well—for all of us. And while a
helpful example is useful in shaping all areas
of our prayer life, we want to focus here on the
prayer of intercession, wherein we experience
the privilege and responsibility of praying for
others and their needs. Few things say as much
about the depth of our care for others as does
our commitment to pray for them. And, as we
saw in chapter 2, this is a ministry in which we
partner with Christ himself—the greatest of all
intercessors.

So, then, what does it look like to intercede in
prayer for others? What does it mean to pray for
one another? In Philippians 1:3–11, the apostle
Paul models for us a wonderful example of
intercession.

If you think about the kinds of prayers we
often pray, you'll probably agree that we tend
to focus on temporal, material, or physical
priorities. Our concern with the externals of life
is not wrong or inappropriate. However, Paul's
model for intercession is strikingly different,

for he overwhelmingly focuses on spiritual
concerns, spiritual goals, and spiritual desires.
And it is a model that we would be wise to
learn, develop, and implement.

Paul's Intercession and Thanksgiving

> I thank my God in all my remem-
> brance of you (Philippians 1:3).

   As Paul opens his letter to the Philippians,
this priority of prayer is foremost in his mind.
His prayers on their behalf are dramatic and
searching and passionate—and reflect how
deeply he loves them. This is not only revealed
in his prayers for them, but also in the way he
describes his prayers for them. As a result, the
apostle gives them (and us) a great model for
praying for the "one anothers" in our lives.
   To fully appreciate Paul's greeting of
thanksgiving—"I thank my God in all my
remembrance of you"—it is helpful to remember
the origins of the assembly of believers at
Philippi and Paul's relationship with them.
Having traversed Asia Minor (modern-day
Turkey) while being prohibited by the Holy Spirit
from speaking the message of Christ along the
way (Acts 16), Paul received a vision in the

night: a man of Macedonia was standing and
appealing to him, and saying, 'Come over to
Macedonia and help us'" (16:9).[B] In response,
he immediately crossed from Turkey into
Greece, where the first believers to be won
to Christ on European soil both heard and
embraced the cross of Christ. A woman named
Lydia had her heart "opened" by the Lord, and
she "and her household" placed their faith in the
Savior and were baptized (16:14–15).[B]

But as Paul and his fellow missionaries
made their way to Lydia's house to establish
a "place of prayer," they were confronted by
a girl possessed by evil spirits, who was then
rescued from the demonic presence in her life
by the power of Christ through Paul's words
to her. Her masters, having lost the profit
they made from the girl as a fortune teller,
pressed charges against Paul and Silas, who
were beaten mercilessly and imprisoned. That
night, however, instead of bemoaning their
mistreatment, "Paul and Silas were praying
and singing hymns of praise to God, and
the prisoners were listening to them," when
suddenly an earthquake shook the prison and
broke open the door and their chains. They then
led the jailer to Christ (16:16–34).[B]

Out of all these events, the church at Philippi was born. And now Paul was writing to this first European congregation from his place of imprisonment in a different city (Rome).

As he begins his letter to them, Paul makes it clear that he is thankful *to* God, and he is thankful *for* them. Clearly, giving thanks to God is a significant part of prayer, because it speaks of a heart of gratitude for the goodness and faithfulness of God. It lifts up and celebrates the trustworthiness of God. In Paul's thanksgiving, however, his gratitude is more targeted. He is thankful for the fledgling community of faith at Philippi, for they are the fruit of his labor and, as a result, the source of his greatest and deepest joy.

Paul's attitude here mirrors the tone of his letter to the congregation at Thessalonica, to whom he wrote, "For who is our hope or joy or crown of exultation? Is it not even you, in the presence of our Lord Jesus at His coming? For you are our glory and joy" (1 Thessalonians 2:19–20). He gratefully celebrates the opportunity to have known them, served them, and helped them in their journey of faith. Paul continues by saying that he gives thanks to God "in *all* my remembrance of you." He tells the Philippians that all of his memories of them

were a source of gratitude to God. That is quite
a statement!

As someone who has pastored three
different churches in three different regions
of the United States, I wish I could tell you
that all of my memories of all of the events
and all of the people in all of those churches
were always a source of gratitude, but I can't.
Pastoral work is a crazy quilt of highs and lows,
with seasons of tremendous joy and times of
fierce disappointment—and I was never beaten
within an inch of my life and wrongly imprisoned
like Paul was in Philippi. It is remarkable that
he could feel so warmly about his time there
that *all* his memories of them were grounds
for thanksgiving. What a unique bond of love
they had, that, even with the difficulties and
challenges he had faced in Philippi, when Paul
thought of his brothers and sisters in Christ
there, his memories were happy ones.

How we remember others is a strategic
part of intercession—but there is a flip side to
that coin. How do people remember us? What
legacy are we leaving? Will people remember
us as difficult, self-centered, and arrogant? Or
will their memories of us elicit thankfulness and
even praise to God for our lives?

Paul's Intercession and Consistency

> I thank my God . . . always offering
> prayer with joy in my every prayer for
> you all, in view of your participation in
> the gospel from the first day until now
> (Philippians 1:3–5). *Bible*

In the movie *Remember the Titans*, football *(Movie)*
coach Herman Boone introduces his new
assistant coaches to their offensive playbook,
which consists of only a handful of plays—a
simple approach unthinkable in today's football
universe. When questioned about the lack of
creativity in his scheme, he simply responds,
"It's like Novocaine. Just give it time; it
always works." Why? Because Coach Boone
intended to drill his players over and over and
over and over on those plays until they could
consistently be executed to perfection. Having
those plays so polished and finely tuned that
they would never break down was critical to the
Titans' success—and it worked. Armed with
those few plays, the Titans won the Virginia
state football title that year. Consistency was
the key.

The apostle Paul's prayers were also
rooted in a commitment to consistency. As

he remembered the Philippians' consistent
participation with him in the spread of
Bible the gospel (v. 5), Paul shared with them
his consistent prayers on their behalf—a
consistency expressed in three critical ways.

"Always"—Paul declared that he was
continually praying for his dear friends. This
reveals not only his love for them, but also his
priorities. He knew that there was nothing more
valuable that he could do for them than to pray.
And it is worth noticing that this was not just
another task on Paul's apostolic to-do list. He
made it clear that it was his great joy to be able
to pray for them and intercede for them.

Intercessory prayer was not only the most
important thing he could do for them, it was
also a source of personal joy and satisfaction
to be able to continue his service to them in his
prayers, even though they were separated by
miles and by his own imprisonment.

"Every"—Next we see that Paul's
commitment to pray for the Philippian believers
was not sporadic or inconsistent. He had a
fervent desire for God's best in their lives—a
desire that resurfaced in his heart every time he
prayed! If "always" speaks of time, then "every"
speaks of opportunity. At every opportunity,

his prayers were lifted to God on their behalf, showing both Paul's commitment to prayer and his devotion to them.

"All"—Paul told the Philippians that he was interceding "for you all." He was not just praying for his pals, or his coffee group, or his golf foursome, or his small group, or the people who said nice things about his sermons. His commitment to prayer was without discrimination or favoritism. He prayed for them all.

Paul confirmed that this had been his practice on their behalf—consistently—"from the first day until now" (v. 5).[B] You can't help *Bible* but see the tenderness of Paul as he looked back, reminiscing from his prison about that first day when he met Lydia, the first converts, and the founding of the church. Imagine the encouragement and comfort those thoughts must have brought his weary heart. Consider all the serving and speaking and mentoring and writing and suffering Paul had endured. Had it been worth it all? At times it may not have seemed like it, but as he remembered how the church at Philippi began, he continued to be driven to thankful prayer on their behalf!

These three elements—always, every, all—are an example of consistency that can not only encourage us as we seek to live for Christ in our community, but also shows that consistency is a key element in the work of intercession. Always. Every. All.

Paul's Intercession and His Motive

> I am confident of this very thing, that
> He who began a good work in you
> will perfect it until the day of Christ
> Jesus. For it is only right for me to
> feel this way about you all, because
> I have you in my heart, since both in
> my imprisonment and in the defense
> and confirmation of the gospel, you
> all are partakers of grace with me. For
> God is my witness, how I long for you
> all with the affection of Christ Jesus
> (Philippians 1:6–8).

In police procedural television dramas, from Law and Order to NCIS, many elements are involved in trying to determine the identity of the killer. These include the physical evidence (ranging from fingerprints to DNA), eyewitness accounts, and opportunity. Does the physical evidence support the theory of a certain person's guilt? Do the witnesses agree, and does their testimony point to that same individual? Did the suspect have the opportunity to commit the crime, or does his alibi stand up against the scrutiny of the investigation? But in every case there is another key element to uncovering the truth: Did the suspect have a motive for committing the crime? Inevitably, some hidden fact is uncovered that gives the detectives the "why" behind the crime. Motive pulls the case together and provides the solution.

Few things are more revealing about our true selves than what motivates us. In fact, the Scriptures continually remind us that why we do what we do is often far more important than what we do. This also relates to prayer and intercession. As we continue to consider Paul's prayers for his friends at Philippi, we discover what drove his prayers and that his motivation was both vertical and horizontal.

Paul's Vertical Motivation

There is no substitute for spiritual confidence, and the apostle makes it clear that he is confident about both the ongoing work that God is doing in their lives and the ultimate outcome of that work (v. 6). He is certain that

God's perfecting work is active in their lives and that this work will come to its fruition at the right time. He is looking forward to the hope of Christ, to the upward call of Christ, and to the completion of the good work that Christ is performing.

Key to this, of course, is where Paul's confidence is grounded, because this displays the difference between "self-confidence" and "Christ-confidence." If we are motivated by self-confidence, we have our warning: "Let him who thinks he stands take heed that he does not fall" (1 Corinthians 10:12). Jesus made it clear (John 15:5), as did Paul (Philippians 4:13), that our confidence must be in Him, not in ourselves. We are to put no confidence in the flesh (Philippians 3:3), but in the Lord, who "will be your confidence and will keep your foot from being caught" (Proverbs 3:26). That will lift our prayers and strengthen our hearts because our confidence is in the God who is able.

And what is "the good work" (Philippians 1:6) of which Paul is confident? It is the ongoing work of growing to maturity in the life of a believer. It is the process by which God takes broken people and makes them whole, and it begins with salvation and continues until the "day of Christ Jesus" when we see Him and are *Bible* fully conformed to His likeness (1 John 3:1–3). *Bible* That is Paul's desire, and it is a desire born out of confidence in both the purposes and the ability of the God to whom he prays on behalf of his friends.

Paul's Horizontal Motivation

While his vertical motivation is his confidence in God, Paul's horizontal motivation is rooted in his deep love for the believers at Philippi. Notice two phrases he uses in Philippians 1:7–8: *Bible*

> "I have you in my heart"
> "I long for you all with the affection of
>   Christ Jesus"

Those phrases display how deeply Paul loved and cared for these people. After all that had happened to Paul and his ministry team in Philippi, that place could easily have been the source of many bad memories—false accusations, imprisonment, beatings. Instead, Paul focused on his deep love and affection for the people there who were following the Master.

What strikes me most about these twin motives—confidence in God and love for his friends—is that they are utterly selfless on the part of Paul. And this offers a compelling challenge for the motivation behind our own prayers. Why do we pray for others? Is it a kind of I-have-to-do-this-to-earn-spiritual-points motivation, or do we sincerely desire to see Christ working in the lives of those for whom we pray?

Paul's Intercession and Love

> And this I pray, that your love may abound still more and more in real knowledge and all discernment, so that you may approve the things that are excellent, in order to be sincere and blameless until the day of Christ; having been filled with the fruit of righteousness which comes through Jesus Christ, to the glory and praise of God (Philippians 1:9–11).[3]

Bible

There are many areas of life for which we should pray—and none of them are off-limits. We certainly should pray for one another in matters of family, health, work, and finances. As I write this, my sister is beginning what will no doubt be a long and challenging battle with breast cancer. Now, and for the foreseeable future, my prayers for her are focused on her strength to withstand the surgeries and treatments. They include prayer for her heart and spirit—that, in the hard times, she won't be discouraged. They include prayer for the medical personnel and for her husband and kids—all of whom face this unwelcome test with her.

Yet as meaningful and important as it is to pray for jobs and family and relationships and health, there is also the deeper reality that needs to be addressed.

As Paul interceded for the Philippians, he went to that deeper reality by praying for their spiritual development. His requests are far from the grocery lists of wants and wishes that often mark our prayers, for they reach into the hearts of his friends and their relationship with God. Notice what Paul prays for on their behalf:

- That their love might abound more and more.
- That their love might be marked by knowledge and discernment.
- That they might be able to reach for the excellent.
- That they might be sincere and blameless in their living for the Savior.

- That the righteousness of Christ might bear
  fruit in their lives for His honor.

Those are high-octane requests. Yet each
of those characteristics or qualities was seen
in Jesus as He walked upon the earth. He
loved passionately, even to the point of going
to the cross for people who were undeserving
of such a gift. His wisdom often amazed the
crowds that gathered to hear Him. Everything
Christ did was done with excellence to reflect
well on His Father. Even the man (Pilate) who
condemned Jesus to the cross had to confess
that he could find no fault in Him. And the
righteousness of Christ was perfectly exhibited
for all to see, again displaying the absolute
perfection of His relationship with the Father.
The desire of Paul's heart was that Christ
would be formed in the Philippians so that their
lives would reflect the heart and character of
the Savior.

Paul was not opposed to praying for the
ordinary, everyday needs of life, but above all
he was committed to praying for believers'
spiritual well-being and was also committed
to helping them work toward it. Paul's passion
for Christ was matched by his passion for their

Christlikeness. His prayers reflect the loftiest of goals and desires, and his example can point our hearts in the right direction as we pray.

Someone Is Praying For You

Paul set the example for intercession with his prayers for the church at Philippi, but, as always, our ultimate example is Christ himself, who "always lives to make intercession" for us (Hebrews 7:25).

When my wife and I were in Bible college, we traveled with one of the singing groups that toured around the country representing the school. During our final year with the group, one of the concerts we did repeatedly was a musical by Lanny Wolfe entitled *Greater Is He*. The music and message combined to declare the power, worthiness, and faithfulness of God, looking at His power revealed in creation, His power displayed on the cross, and the wonder of Christ's incarnation and the intimacy of God's presence in the lives of those who come to Him through faith. *Greater Is He* expresses some of the most worshipful ideas I have ever heard put to music.

Yet in the midst of all this praise and worship was a song that, at first glance, might have seemed out of place. It simply said, "Someone is praying for you." Though the lyrics of the song were simple, the message was profound. Someone—Jesus Christ—is engaged in intercession for us, and, when we pray for one another, we join with Him in that matchless privilege.

Someone in heaven and many someones on earth pray for us. Now, the question remains—for whom will you and I pray?

Talking Together About Intercession

- Who have been strong spiritual examples or influences in your life? Were the examples positive or negative? Did those examples also model prayer for you?
- Paul repeatedly lifts up the Philippians with requests that seem to be of a higher nature than our prayers often reach. How are his requests different from ours? Is it possible to blend both together in interceding for others? If so, how?
- In Philippians 1, Paul unveiled both his vertical and horizontal motivations for praying for the believers at Philippi. What were those motivations? Why are they important?

- How do those motives reflect selflessness in Paul's prayers?
- What does Christ's never-ceasing intercession on your behalf as His child say about His love for you? His commitment to you? His investment in you?

LET'S TALK ABOUT

MYSTERY

Agatha Christie is regarded as one of the best mystery writers of all time. Her stories are filled with twists and turns, leading to heart-pounding suspense that holds you in its grasp until the very end when the mystery is solved.

I got a firsthand taste of Christie's expertise when, in high school, I worked on the drama club's production of *Ten Little Indians*. The plot *(DRAMA SHOW)* is simple. Ten people are invited to a secluded retreat where, one by one, they are murdered. As each victim falls, one less suspect is available, until finally the murderer is exposed. It is a brilliantly told tale that truly fulfills our idea of the word *mystery*, with clues pointing first in one direction and then another.

But for people who came to our modest production of the play, it was an even greater mystery. Why? Because we changed the ending! Those who came not knowing the ending beforehand still had all of Agatha Christie's spine-tingling drama, but those who came to the program already familiar with the story had an extra layer of mystery added when the story did not resolve as they had expected. It was great fun and helped to make me a huge fan of good mysteries.

When it comes to prayer, however, a different kind of mystery is involved—namely, how does prayer actually work? This sense of mystery was awakened in my own heart while I was in Bible college. Our pastor would frequently say, "Nothing of eternal value is ever accomplished apart from prayer." I heard him make that remark hundreds of times (seriously, it was hundreds of times), and, as a young believer, I found comfort in that statement. It seemed so direct and clear, so right—and it is. But that does not mean that it is *simple*. In fact, prayer can at times seem a mystery, for it raises a theological dilemma:

- **God is sovereign**. God is in control of the universe, and His purposes are sure and settled.
- **The believer's prayers matter**. We are told in the Bible that our prayers matter and that we are to join in with God in His work and purposes because our prayers are powerful.

How do we resolve these two things that seem so contradictory? If God is sovereign and everything is already planned according to His purposes, how can our prayers matter?

The Sovereignty of God

Before 1982, many people had never heard of the Falkland Islands in the southern Atlantic Ocean. Resting about 250 miles east of the South American coastline, the Falklands consist of less than 4,700 square miles but were the site of what is now remembered as the Falklands War or the Falklands Crisis.

Argentina has claimed sovereignty over the islands since the 1800s, even though the British have controlled them. Then, on April 2, 1982, Argentina invaded the islands to assert its claim over the territory. Margaret Thatcher, then the British prime minister, responded by sending troops and naval forces from the United Kingdom and drove the Argentinians out—at the cost of over 900 lives lost and almost 2,000 injured.

To those watching from the outside, it seemed like much ado about nothing. This small set of islands didn't seem worthy of such a conflict. But that wasn't the point. The

Falklands War was not simply about property or a land grab; it was about sovereignty. To this day, more than thirty years later, there is still tension between Argentina and the United Kingdom over the Falklands, and there has not been a final resolution as to who has the right to rule there.

When it comes to sovereignty over the world and all creation, the Scriptures make it clear that no such dispute exists. The Creator has reserved that right to himself. His rule, while resisted and disregarded by much of this planet, is nevertheless firmly in hand. How complete is His authority? In Isaiah 46:9–10, we hear the Sovereign Lord declare:

> "Remember the former things long past,
> For I am God, and there is no other;
> I am God, and there is no one like Me,
> Declaring the end from the beginning,
> And from ancient times things which have
>   not been done,
> Saying, 'My purpose will be established,
> And I will accomplish all My good
>   pleasure.'"

Packed into that ancient declaration are important keys to God's rightful sovereignty. He declares, "I am God, and there is no other." He alone reigns supreme in heaven and on earth, and His authority, which is unquestioned in heaven, should be unquestioned on earth as well—as Jesus taught us to pray in Matthew 6 with the words, "Your will be done, on earth as it is in heaven." Isaiah also tells us that not only is He God, He is utterly unique—"there is no one like Me." This uniqueness supports God's position as the Sovereign One:

Only He can declare the end from the beginning—for He is timeless.
Only He can declare things yet undone— for He is omniscient.
Only He can accomplish *all* of His purposes and *all* of His own good pleasure—for He is sovereign ruler of heaven and earth.

When we pray, we are not praying to a weak, undecided being who is wringing his hands and hoping everything will turn out okay in the end. We are praying to the sovereign Ruler of heaven and earth who is working to accomplish His ultimate ends for our good and for His own honor, and who will accomplish His purposes in His time and in His way.

The Participation of the Believer

Anyone who knows me knows that I'm passionate about sports, so it is a lot of fun for me to be part of the Sports Spectrum radio team. Talking about sports and using them as a bridge to take people from the games they love to the Christ they need is a great privilege. As we discuss various sports on the program, we will occasionally discuss the current popularity of different sports and which one is the current "king of the hill" in the sports world. For years, baseball was regarded as "the great American pastime." But today, every poll and survey tells us that the National Football League is now America's favorite. Or is it?

If we are going to accurately answer that question, we must first set some parameters. When we start talking about favorite sports, are we talking about spectator sports or participation sports? The data supports the fact that the most popular *spectator* sport is NFL football, but surveys show that the most popular *participation* sport is walking, followed closely by swimming; and among *team* sports, slow pitch softball is one of the top sports in America. People of all ages—men and women, boys and girls—play softball in city recreation leagues, church leagues, weekend tournaments, and just-for-fun pickup games. For many, the appeal of being able to participate is much more inviting than just sitting and watching others compete.

Likewise, the life of faith is not a spectator activity; it is all about participation—and nowhere is this more true than in the matter of prayer. When we pray, we participate with the sovereign God by joining with Him in His plans and purposes. The New Testament writer James made this clear when he declared:

> The effective prayer of a righteous man can accomplish much. Elijah was a man with a nature like ours, and he prayed earnestly that it would not rain, and it did not rain on the earth for three years and six months. Then he prayed again, and the sky poured rain and the earth produced its fruit (James 5:16–18).

Bible

Elijah was not a superhero or a larger-than-life figure. Yes, he was called to be a prophet of God, but he was also an ordinary man who was willing to accept that calling—willing to get off the sidelines and get into the game. How?

By praying. James says that Elijah was a man
like us, yet his prayers had impact beyond
imagining. And in this text, James cites one
instance of that impact.

Ahab and his queen, Jezebel, had
plunged the northern kingdom of Israel into
institutionalized idolatry—a condition that God
had promised to judge with drought, which was
devastating for an agrarian culture. Moses had
warned the people about this kind of judgment
centuries before:

> "Beware that your hearts are not de-
> ceived, and that you do not turn away
> and serve other gods and worship
> them. Or the anger of the LORD will be
> kindled against you, and He will shut
> up the heavens so that there will be
> no rain and the ground will not yield
> its fruit; and you will perish quickly
> from the good land which the LORD is
> giving you" (Deuteronomy 11:16–17).[B]

And what was the trigger for that drought?
Elijah. Elijah prayed and the rain was withheld
for three and a half years. Once the divine
discipline had accomplished its task, Elijah

prayed again and the rains returned, quenching
the thirst of the dry and barren farmlands.

But Elijah offers us other examples of the
effective nature of prayer. When he prayed for
the dead son of the widow of Zarephath, "the
life of the child returned to him and he revived"
(1 Kings 17:22). And during the "battle of the *Bible*
gods" on Mount Carmel, Elijah prayed and fire
fell from heaven (1 Kings 18). His confidence *Bible*
in the sovereign purposes of God was so
profound by this point that the prophet did not
even ask for the fire to fall. Instead, Elijah simply
called on the God of the universe to honor
himself so that the people would be drawn back
to Him in repentance.

Elijah was no spectator. He was fully engaged
in the battle for his generation's faith and trust
in God. Could God have done all of that without
him? Certainly. But the sovereign Lord chose
to allow Elijah to take part in the work that He
intended to do—and He calls us to that same
privilege as well.

Paul said that we are God's "fellow workers"
(1 Corinthians 3:9). Why? Because we *Bible*
participate with Him in seeing His purposes
accomplished in the world, and we do that, in
part, as we pray.

James was right. The effective prayer of a righteous person can accomplish much.

The Value of Mystery

So then, how do we reconcile the sovereignty of God with the power of prayer? Some say that this is a hopeless contradiction. But it is not a contradiction. It is a mystery. Where we can get into trouble is when we try to undo that mystery instead of allowing it simply to be.

I once heard a Bible teacher assert that when he teaches on salvation, if the text speaks of God's sovereignty and election, he preaches that concept as if it were the only one in the Bible. He went on to say that he handles man's free will the same way—as if it were the only biblical truth on the subject. At first glance that seems to have merit, but is it the wisest approach to biblical mystery? How can we attempt to understand either sovereignty or free will unless we do so in the context of both?

It has often been said that any truth taken to an extreme can become a form of heresy. This also can occur when we ignore the balancing elements of the Bible's story of God's dealings with men and women. If we fail to do this, we are likely to lose our balance. In fact, failure to balance both truths—God's sovereignty and our participation—can actually lead to a warped and unhealthy view of prayer.

Pushing too hard on the side of God's *sovereignty* can lead followers of Christ to become apathetic or even fatalistic about the value of prayer, saying, "Why should I even bother to pray if God is going to do whatever He wants anyway?"

Pushing too hard on our *participation* in prayer can cause believers to think that their prayers must direct and determine the outcomes for which they pray, even to the point of manipulating God himself.

The key, of course, is to allow for balance between these two. This is the fundamental reality and the mystery of prayer: God is in control and will accomplish all His purposes in the world; and, at the same time, the effective prayer of righteous men and women makes a difference. When we humbly allow for this mystery, we learn to rest in His wisdom and trust His resolution of the things we cannot sort out on our own. We leave it in His hands.

Why is mystery a good and wonderful thing? Because it reminds us of the greatness of our God. He cannot be squeezed into our theological cubbyholes. He cannot be defined by theological terminology or creeds. Rather than causing us to fear or doubt, mystery should bring a great sense of relief and peace. He is, and He is God. And He is the God who is beyond our imagination, let alone our classifications. As we read in Isaiah:[B]

> "For My thoughts are not your thoughts,
> Nor are your ways My ways," declares the
>   LORD.
> "For as the heavens are higher than the
>   earth,
> So are My ways higher than your ways
> And My thoughts than your thoughts"
>   (55:8–9)[B]

Bible

The God of mystery calls us to trust Him and rest in Him and depend upon Him and, yes, join Him in His work. He is a God worth serving. He is a God worth knowing. And He is a God with whom we can entrust our prayers. Mystery and all.

> Immortal, invisible, God only wise,
> In light inaccessible hid from our eyes,
> Most blessed most glorious, the Ancient of
>   Days,

Almighty, victorious, Thy great name we
praise.

—Walter C. Smith

Talking Together About Mystery

- Do you find mysteries intriguing or frustrating? Why?
- Think about the statement that any truth taken to an extreme can become a form of heresy. What examples of that have you seen?
- When you think about the sovereignty of God, do you feel a sense of comfort or a sense of despair? How has that response influenced your attitude toward prayer?
- Why does the thought of seeking to manipulate God in prayer work against a life of faith? What does such a thought say about us? What does it say about our view of God?
- Instead of being a source of frustration, having a God who embodies a measure of mystery should be a source of comfort. What is the reason given for that comfort? Do you agree or disagree? Why?

LET'S TALK ABOUT

CONFIDENCE

A heartbroken father had brought his demon-possessed son to Jesus, only to find the Rabbi absent and His disciples unable to cure the boy. Their failure generated accusations from the ever-present attack force of the religious establishment—a discussion that was ongoing when Jesus arrived on the scene. After seeing the demon throw the boy to the ground in a seizure of pain and horror, Christ turned His attention to the father, probing his heart and allowing him to speak of the years of hurt, struggle, and impotence that he had felt as he watched his child suffer, yet was unable to help him. When the issue of faith became the pointed end of the probe, the father replied to Jesus's questions with an answer burdened by the weight of both grief and despair, emptiness and honesty: "I do believe; help my unbelief" (Mark 9:24). *Bible*

How many of us can echo this father's honest words? Torn between faith and doubt, belief and unbelief? Believing, yet sometimes wrestling with doubts? Unlike that devastated father, however, we are often less open and honest about our doubts. Cloaking ourselves in religious verbiage, we erect the façade of the faithful, all the while knowing in our hearts that our struggle goes beyond the particulars of whatever crisis we are facing and reaches to the essence of our walk with Christ.

Do we trust Him?

Can we trust Him?

Will we trust Him?

We believe, but are silently stretched on the rack of unbelief. So, how do we respond? That may vary from moment to moment and circumstance to circumstance, so maybe a better question is this: How *would* we respond if doubt were replaced with confidence—not in ourselves, but in the Christ we have trusted to secure our eternity?

Well, first we must have a basis for that confidence. It cannot be just warm feelings and happy thoughts. It must be a muscular assurance rooted in the One whose grace truly is sufficient and whose strength is mighty. And it must also be rooted in relationship with Him if we are to understand how to pray confidently, even when our faith is stretched.

Why is the relationship element so vital? In the previous chapter we celebrated the fact that God is sovereign. He is the absolute Ruler of the universe. Yet this truth sometimes causes misunderstanding about prayer. When relationship enters the picture, we realize that prayer is not a subordinate going to his commander for marching orders. Prayer is a hurting child turning to the Father who loves him or her. Thus, confidence in prayer begins with the profound understanding that God has powerful concern for His child. This is at the core of our confidence, and it is laid out for us in Hebrews 4:15–16. *Bible*

> For we do not have a high priest who cannot sympathize with our weaknesses, but One who has been tempted in all things as we are, yet without sin. Therefore, let us draw near with confidence to the throne of grace, so that we may receive mercy and find grace to help in time of need.

This is the nature of the God to whom we pray, the nature of the Son and His care for His flock. We "draw near with confidence to the throne of grace"—we pray—because of who God is and how much He loves us.

Confidence in God's Care

It had been a long day of ministry filled with the demands and needs of hurting people. In fact, it had been such an exhausting day that the fully human Son of God had fallen deeply asleep in a boat as He and the disciples crossed the Sea of Galilee. As Jesus slept, a storm began brewing on the small lake that was home to the Galilean fishing community. Panicked by the severity of the storm and the possibility that it would sink the small fishing boat, the disciples roused the sleeping Savior. Seeing His unconcern, they asked an interesting question:

Bible   "Teacher, do You not care that we are perishing?" (Mark 4:38).

On another occasion, Jesus was visiting with His friends Martha, Mary, and Lazarus. As He taught, Mary sat at His feet, "listening to His *Bible* word" (Luke 10:39). Martha, however, who was busy preparing to feed those who had gathered to hear Jesus, was weary of Mary ignoring the work. Martha asked Jesus to intervene, saying:

> "Lord, do You not care that my sister
> has left me to do all the serving alone?
> Then tell her to help me" (Luke 10:40). *Bible*

In each instance, what was in question was not the storm on the sea or the work of meal preparation. What was in question was whether or not Jesus *cared* about the storm or the work. What was in question was whether or not His followers could have confidence that their Master was genuinely concerned about the things that concerned them. And we might ask the same about those things that concern us.

The writer of the letter to the Hebrews steps in to assure us that we can have confidence that He cares.

> For we do not have a high priest
> who cannot sympathize with our
> weaknesses, but One who has been
> tempted in all things as we are, yet
> without sin (4:15). *Bible*

This is part of the great value of the incarnation of Christ. He lived on this earth. He experienced hunger, fatigue, hatred, misunderstanding, and struggle. And He did so in order to be able to show us a vitally important

Bible truth: He knows how we feel. Hebrews 4:15[B]
reminds us that He was tested like we are and
knows the struggles we face. He cared enough
to walk this life in this world so that He could be
an understanding priest to us.

This statement would have shocked the
Hebrew readers of this letter, for, in the
first century, the priesthood had become a
vested aristocracy—wealthy, privileged, and
removed from the common people and their
daily struggles. Jesus was just the opposite.
As a result, we do not go to a distant high
priest separated from us by social status or
ecclesiastical authority. We go to the Christ,
who cares for us with all His heart, and who
proved it by living among us.

Not only did He prove His care by living
among us; He proved it by dying for us.
Perhaps the greatest shadowy place of our
doubts is not that we don't believe in God, but
that we don't recognize just how deeply and
passionately the Father loves His children. Paul
told the church at Rome that our God cares so
deeply that He did not spare His own Son in
Bible coming to our rescue (Romans 8:32).[B]

Does it seem that He has suddenly stopped
caring? One look at the cross is all that is

needed to remind us of the Christ who came and lived and died and rose again because of how much He cares.

> Does Jesus care when my heart is pained
> Too deeply for mirth or song,
> As the burdens press, and the cares
>   distress,
> And the way grows weary and long?
>
> Oh, yes, He cares, I know He cares,
> His heart is touched with my grief;
> When the days are weary, the long nights
>   dreary,
> I know my Savior cares.

—Frank E. Graeff

Confidence in God's Power

When I was about fourteen, I delivered newspapers to earn a little pocket money. One day in my hometown in West Virginia, as I finished working my paper route, a car filled with older teenagers went flying past me going fast—way too fast. They must have been going nearly 80 miles an hour in a 35 MPH zone. As they got to the next block, suddenly a car pulled out of a side street and the two cars crashed. I ran to the scene and saw bodies on the street and hanging from the cars. Two dead, seven injured.

I had never seen a dead body before. I had never witnessed such carnage in my young life. And that was the problem—I was the only witness. The police arrived and asked what happened. Then, over the following months, I gave depositions to lawyers and insurance companies. It was overwhelming! I was absolutely certain of what I had seen, but at my young age, I had no confidence in my ability to tell the story for all these people who kept asking questions and probing for inconsistencies. As a result, I had no confidence that I was able to deal with the forces that were confronting me. I was outmatched.

The three young men who were brought before King Nebuchadnezzar might have felt outmatched too, for they knew one thing with certainty—their lives were on the line. They had defied the royal decree to bow and worship the image that Nebuchadnezzar had raised to himself, and now they faced the king himself to answer for their defiance. As the king confronted them, his tirade was not only at them, but also at their God, for that was their reason for not bowing before the image. The king offered them both a second chance and a threat:

> "Now if you are ready, at the moment you hear the sound of the horn, flute, lyre, trigon, psaltery and bagpipe and all kinds of music, to fall down and worship the image that I have made, very well. But if you do not worship, you will immediately be cast into the midst of a furnace of blazing fire; and what god is there who can deliver you out of my hands?" (Daniel 3:15).[3]   *Bible*

There it is. The question that Nebuchadnezzar thought would end all opposition: "What god is there . . . ." It was rhetorical, of course, for the king fully believed that there was no god able to resist his greatness. But Hananiah, Mishael, and Azariah (better known as Shadrach, Meshach, and Abednego) were confident in their God, causing them to respond:

> "O Nebuchadnezzar, we do not need to give you an answer concerning this matter. If it be so, our God whom we serve is able to deliver us from the

furnace of blazing fire; and He will deliver us out of your hand, O king. But
even if He does not, let it be known to
you, O king, that we are not going to
serve your gods or worship the gold-
en image that you have set up" (Daniel 3:16–18).[B]

Bible
Bible

Not only were they confident in their God's
presence, they were also confident in their
God's ability to handle the life-or-death
moment in which they found themselves. This
was not a confidence in their own ability to
believe or trust or perform under pressure. It
was a complete confidence in the ability of God
to deal with the daunting circumstances and
the danger they faced.

These contrasting pictures reveal the
challenge we face in prayer. Sometimes we feel
that confidence should be rooted in what we
can do and how we can perform, but nothing
could be further from the truth. The confidence
that we carry into our prayers is not in ourselves
or our faith or our skill as pray-ers. Nor is it a
confidence that everything is going to work out
as we have planned, hoped, or desired. It is
confidence that God is able and that His ability

guarantees that His purposes will ultimately be accomplished. It is confidence that in our God we can find help. That is what the writer to the Hebrews affirmed when he wrote:

> Therefore let us draw near with confidence to the throne of grace, so that we may receive mercy and find grace to help in time of need (Hebrews 4:16). *Bible*

When we go to the Lord in prayer ("the throne of grace"), we find Him more than sufficient for the heartaches, challenges, disappointments, and pains of life. We can trust in that because our trust is in Him. And that *trust* is key—because trust is the opposite of worry! In Matthew 6, Jesus repeatedly *Bible* challenges us, "Do not worry!" Over and over He repeats that theme. Then Paul reaffirms it: "Be anxious for nothing!" (Philippians 4:6). And *Bible* Peter adds his voice to the chorus, saying that we are to be "casting all [our] anxiety on Him, because He cares for [us]" (1 Peter 5:7). Instead *Bible* of giving in to fear or doubt or worry or anxiety, we go to God in prayer with confidence that He is more than enough for whatever we are facing.

The fact is, however, that the dual ideas of God's deep care and His sovereign

power challenge us to the core of our being.
Sometimes we don't see how His love can be
real if His power doesn't move in to prevent
tragedy or pain. God does not always seem to
act on His love, and in a broken world, that can
rob us of our hope and trust.

Nobel Prize–winning author Elie Weisel
described his own wrestling match with the
seemingly paradoxical principles of God's love
and God's power in his book *Night*, where he
described the feelings he had as a twelve-year-
old boy imprisoned in the Auschwitz-Birkenau
death camp:

> Never shall I forget that night—the
> first night in the camp—which has
> turned my life into one long night,
> seven times cursed and seven
> times sealed. Never shall I forget the
> smoke. Never shall I forget the faces
> of the children whose bodies I saw
> turned into wreaths of smoke beneath
> a silent blue sky. Never shall I forget
> those flames which consumed my
> faith forever.

Rabbi Harold Kushner, author of *When Bad
Things Happen to Good People*, also struggled

with these contrasting ideas following the death
of his son. Because he could not reconcile
God's goodness and God's power in the face
of tragedy, he redefined God in terms he could
accept and reconcile in his own heart—seeing
God as all-loving but not all-powerful. His pain
could not accept a God who is both.

I have never experienced what Weisel
experienced in the death camp. I have never
lost a child. For that reason, I speak only with
compassion about those who have endured
the worst kinds of pain and heartache. But the
losses, grief, failures, and struggles of life do
not erase the character of God. They either
drive us to Him or propel us away from Him.

God cares deeply for our hurts, and He is
able to do something about them—but always
according to His purposes. And while He may
seem silent in our seasons of struggle, He is
not removed from them. As the prophet Isaiah
foretold of the coming Savior:

> He was despised and forsaken of men,
> A man of sorrows and acquainted with
>   grief;
> And like one from whom men hide their
>   face

He was despised, and we did not esteem
    Him.
Surely our griefs He Himself bore,
And our sorrows He carried;
Yet we ourselves esteemed Him stricken,
Smitten of God, and afflicted.
But He was pierced through for our
    transgressions,
He was crushed for our iniquities,
The chastening for our well-being fell upon
    Him,
And by His scourging we are healed (Isaiah
    53:3–5).[B]

Not only did Jesus come to rescue us from
our sins, struggles, and sorrows, He came
to bear them—and the great, abiding, eternal
evidence of that is the cross of Christ where
God suffered for me and for you. It is the cross
that bridges the gap between God's unlimited
power and God's reaching love. It is the cross
that reminds us that God's power and care are
eternally proven, which prompted John Stott to
write: "I could never myself believe in God, if it
were not for the cross. The only God I believe
in is the one Nietzsche ridiculed as 'God on the

cross.' In a world of real pain, how could one worship a God who was immune to it?"

We can have confidence in this: God does care and He is able, even when we suffer and don't understand why. When His ways don't make sense, we rest in the love and power He displayed on the cross, because that cross is the ultimate and undeniable evidence that He *does* care about us and that He *is* able to do something about our shame and sin and despair and pain. As Charles Wesley wrote:

> Amazing love! how can it be
> That Thou, my God, should die for me?

Confidence in God's Help

In December of 1970, John Lennon gave a landmark interview to *Rolling Stone* magazine in which he worked very hard to demythologize the Beatles. In a poignant moment in the interview, Lennon was asked which of the songs he had written were his favorites. Interestingly, "Help" was on his very short list. He explained that the reason he liked that song so much was the honesty of the lyrics, which form an almost primal cry for help from someone who is deeply hurting. He said he liked it because it was him asking for help.

Unfortunately, Lennon's cry for help seems undirected. Just a cry into the darkness, rather than a calling out to the One who actually *could* help him.

When we go to God in prayer, we do so because we are confident that He can help. That help does not always take the shape we might have chosen or anticipated, but, as we *Bible* have seen, the writer of Hebrews (4:16) makes it clear that when we go to God's throne, we can be confident of His help. Why?

> Because of His invitation to us—"let us draw near with confidence."
> Because of His heart for us—"to the throne of grace" (not judgment).
> Because of His promise to us—"so that we may receive mercy and grace to *help* in time of need."

When we pray, we are merely going where we have been invited—invited by the God who cares for us more deeply and understands us more profoundly than we can ever begin to grasp. And we come to the God who is able to do something about our every concern and need.

It is often the very absence of that confidence that discourages us from praying. And the irony is that this lack of confidence keeps us from the very vehicle (prayer) that God has provided so that we *can* have confidence. In fact, Jesus taught His followers a parable about prayer for that purpose: "Now He was telling them a parable to show that at all times they ought to pray and not to lose heart" (Luke 18:1). In this parable He told them of a widow who was being treated unjustly, but hearing her cries for help, the judge intervened on her behalf.

> And the Lord said, "Hear what the unrighteous judge said; now, will not God bring about justice for His elect who cry to Him day and night, and will He delay long over them?" (Luke 18:6–7).

Jesus's point was that if this woman could have confidence that she could get a hearing and help from an unjust judge, how much more should we have confidence in the God who is altogether righteous in all that He does. How much more can we trust Him to come to our aid as we cry out to Him for help. That is the core of our confidence—God cares, God is able, and

He is very much engaged in the deepest needs
of our hearts.

It is in the spirit of that same confidence
that William Walford long ago wrote words that
continue to stir our trust and confidence in our
God today:

> Sweet hour of prayer! sweet hour of prayer!
> That calls me from a world of care,
> And bids me at my Father's throne
> Make all my wants and wishes known.
> In seasons of distress and grief,
> My soul has often found relief,
> And oft escaped the tempter's snare
> By thy return, sweet hour of prayer!

Talking Together About Confidence

- In what areas of life do you feel a level
  of confidence? In what ways can this
  confidence be positive? In what ways can it
  be negative?

- As you read about Elie Weisel and Harold
  Kuschner, what were your reactions?
  In what ways could you relate to their
  despair? In what ways could you not
  relate?

- The question, "Lord, don't you care?" is often echoed in human experience. Why is it often our first response to tragedy? Why do we find it so natural to question God's love for us?

- In balancing God's care and God's ability, how does the cross represent the perfect marriage of both truths?

- Prayer is not just an activity we have been instructed to perform; it is an invitation into the presence of God. In what ways can that invitation encourage us to be more determined to pray and not to lose heart?

HEART AND SOUL

As followers of Christ, we pray a lot.

We pray before, and sometimes after, our meals.

We pray before we begin meetings and church services.

We pray when we end meetings and church services.

We pray about elections.

We pray for those in government.

We pray about opportunities and failures.

We pray about life.

We pray a lot.

We have been trained and conditioned to pray to such a degree that prayer can become

a "religious thing" we do mechanically without
thought or heart or connection. It can become
a form of the very "meaningless repetition"
Bible that Jesus warned us about in Matthew 6. He
warned us that repeating phrases and using
religious vocabulary is not the heart and soul of
prayer. And He then gave us His own model for
Bible the elements of true prayer (6:9–15):

- Prayer recognizes the worthiness and
  wonder of the God to whom we pray.
- Prayer embraces His kingdom rule in our
  lives for all the tomorrows that stretch
  before us.
- Prayer seeks and receives His provision for
  our needs.
- Prayer understands that our communion with
  Him (and others) is affected by repentance
  and forgiveness—or the lack thereof.
- Prayer sees the dangers of life and gladly
  submits to His gracious rescue from the
  Enemy and from our own brokenness.

Christ's example lifts us to the best place to
begin our prayers:

We begin with His greatness, not our wants.

His purposes, not our goals.

His rule, not our demands.

His protection, not our self-sufficiency.

We begin by being reminded that He is God and we are not, for nothing will shape our communion with the Father quite like a fresh awareness of the One to whom we speak.

We begin by cultivating the heart and soul of a life of prayer that appreciates the wonder of this remarkable privilege.

We begin by seeking His aid even to be able to pray for His help.

We begin by beginning.

So, let's talk!

Let's talk to the God who made us, loves us, rescues us, and desires to form Christ in us.

Let's pray.

Help us get the word out!

Our Daily Bread Publishing exists to feed the soul with the Word of God.

If you appreciated this book, please let others know.

- Pick up another copy to give as a gift.
- Share a link to the book or mention it on social media.
- Write a review on your blog, on a book-seller's website, or at our own site (ourdailybreadpublishing.org).
- Recommend this book for your church, book club, or small group.

Connect with us:

- @ourdailybread
- @ourdailybread
- @ourdailybread

Our Daily Bread Publishing
PO Box 3566
Grand Rapids, Michigan 49501 USA

✉ books@odb.org